A Snarky Adult Coloring Book for

Human Resource Professionals

PADAREX

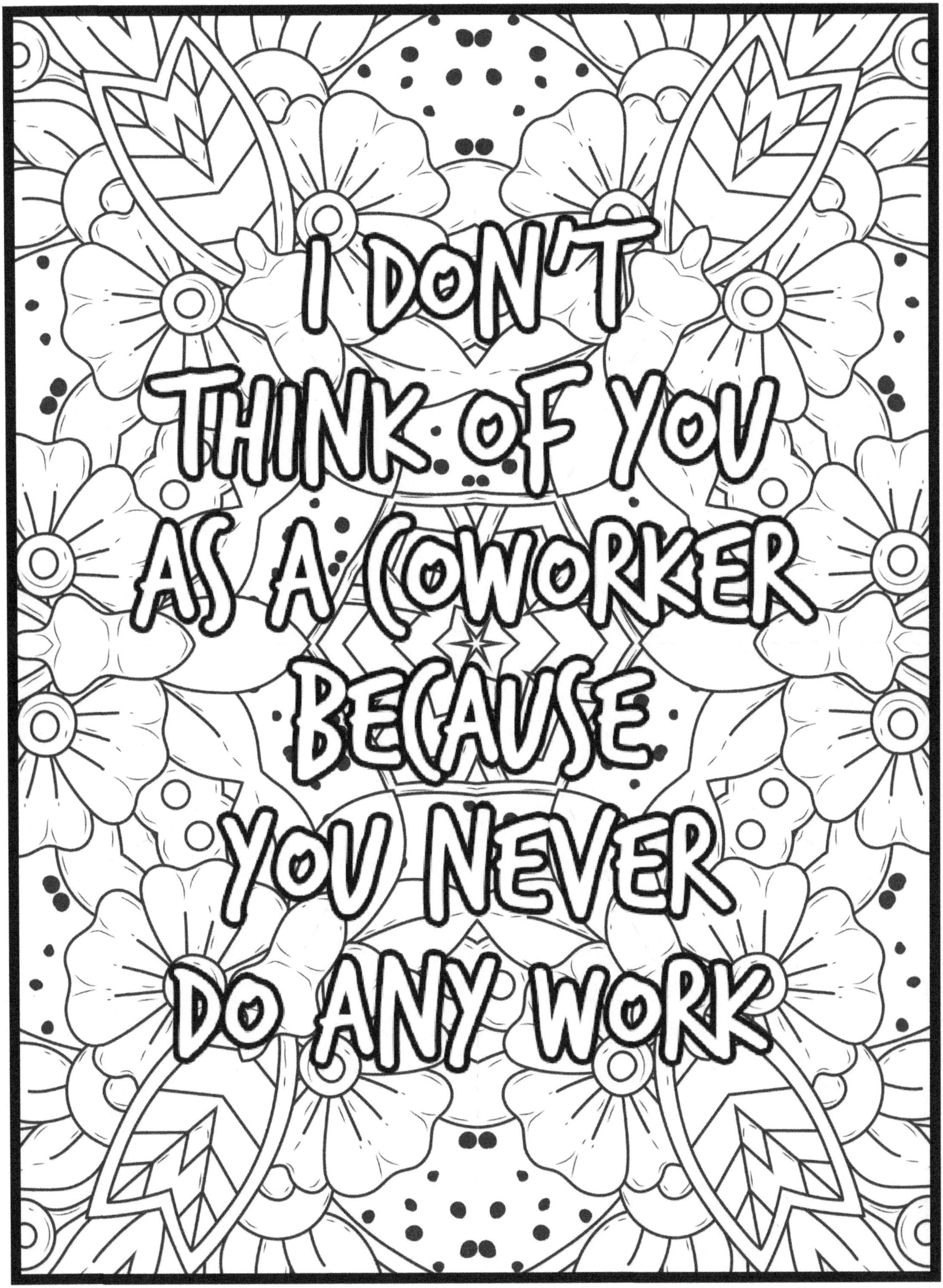
I DON'T
THINK OF YOU
AS A COWORKER
BECAUSE
YOU NEVER
DO ANY WORK

I'M SORRY,
WE CAN'T
HIRE YOU
BUT YOUR
BACKGROUND CHECK
WAS HILAROUS

HR SPECIALIST
BECAUSE
MIRACLE WORKER
ISN'T
AN OFFICIAL
JOB TITLE

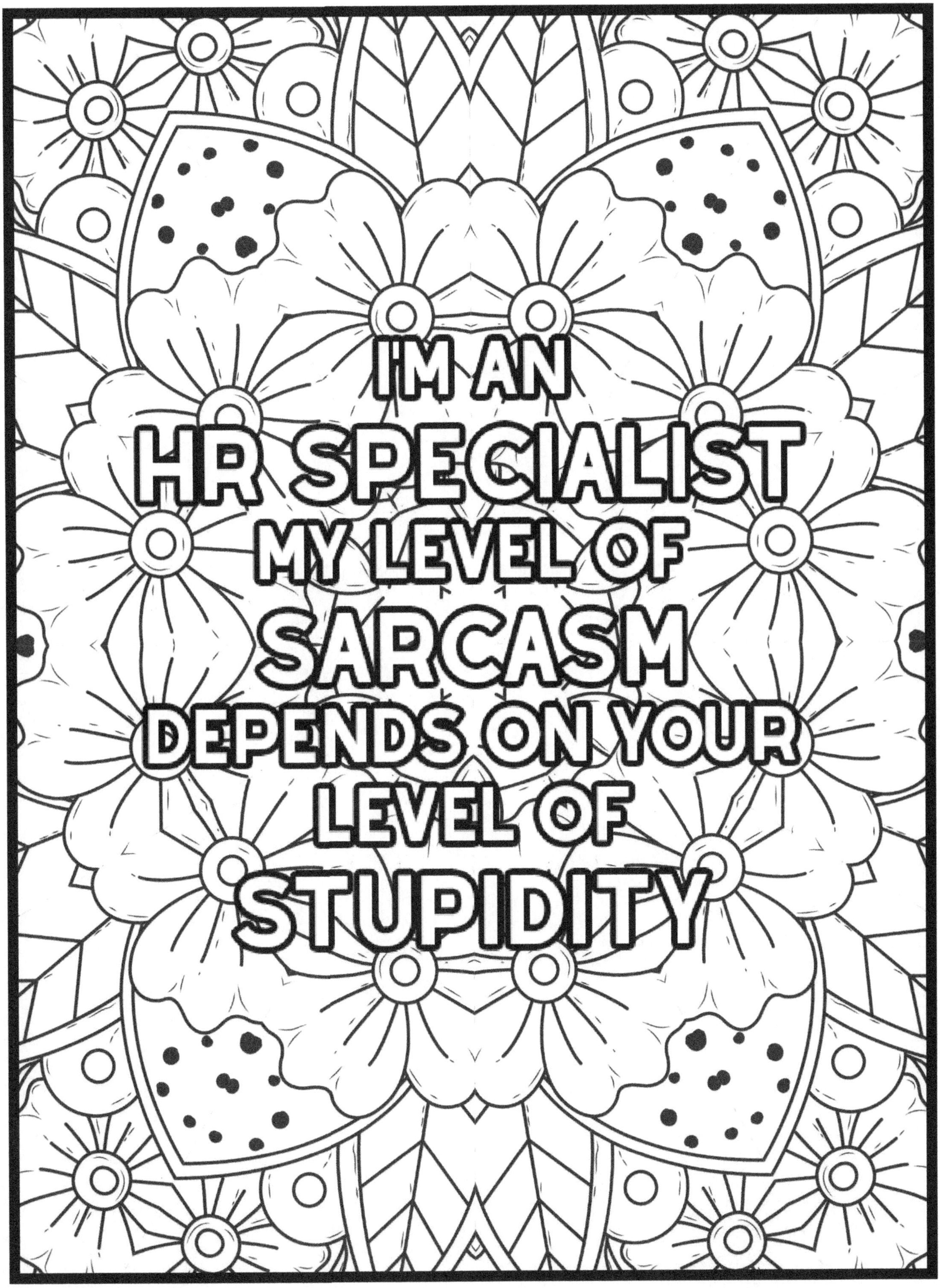
I'M AN
HR SPECIALIST
MY LEVEL OF
SARCASM
DEPENDS ON YOUR
LEVEL OF
STUPIDITY

I'M SILENTLY
JUDGING
YOUR CV

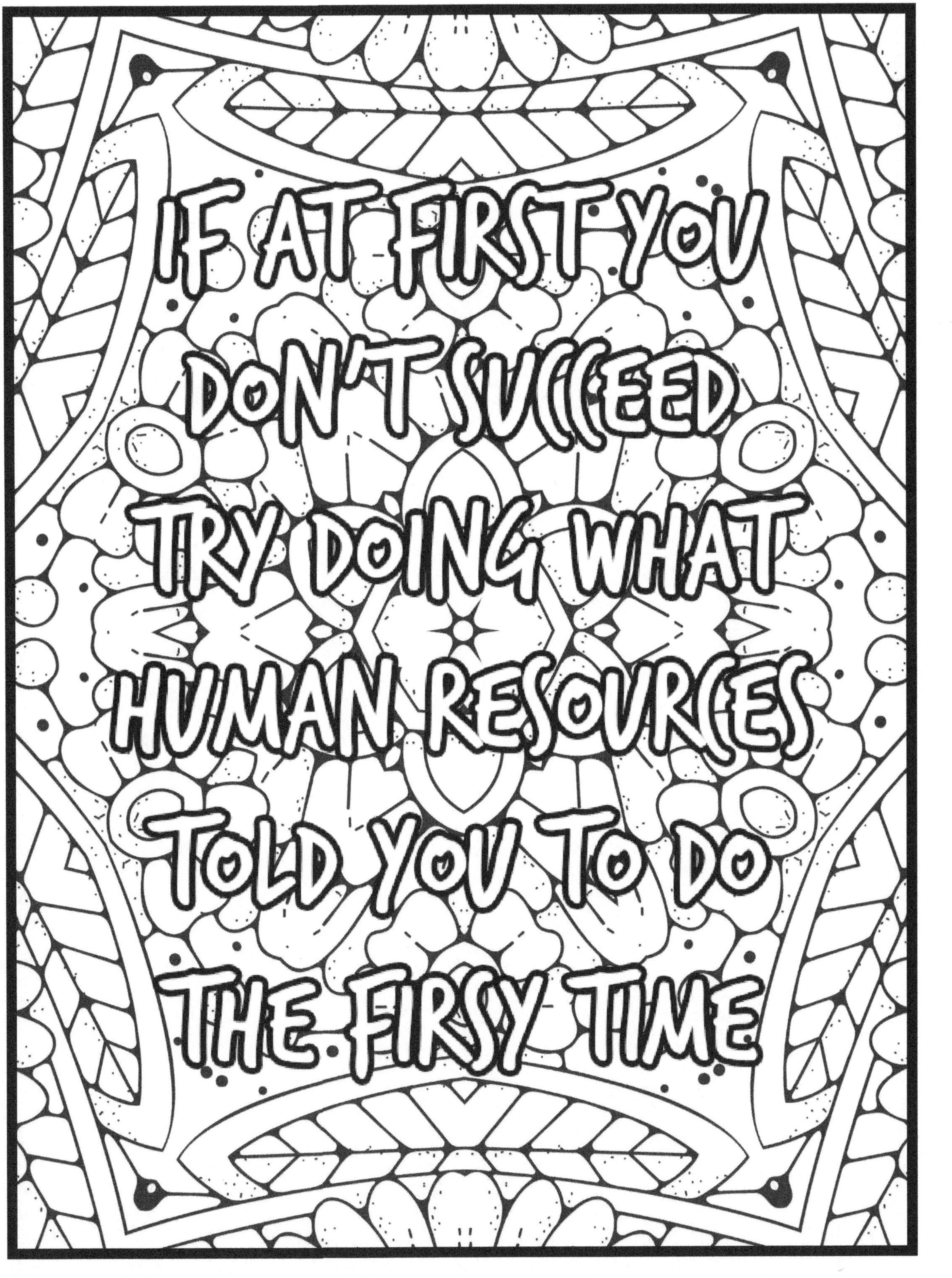
IF AT FIRST YOU
DON'T SUCCEED
TRY DOING WHAT
HUMAN RESOURCES
TOLD YOU TO DO
THE FIRSY TIME

I'm a good
Human
Resources,
I just
cuss a lot

YOU CAN'T
SPELL
HERO
WITHOUT
HR

Sure,
let me drop
everything
and work
on your
problem

May you never
run out of
HR-approved
ways to tell
coworkers
theyre stupid.

If it's really
funny, it's
probably
harassment

I'm not like
regular HR
I'm a
cool HR

I need
stronger
swear words
for this job

THERE'S
NO CRYING
IN HR

HR
THE UNOFFICIAL
PSYCOLOGIST
EVENT PLANNER
PEACEMAKERS

AS AN
HR
PRROFESSIONAL
I TAKE
JUDGING PEOPLE
VERY SERIOUSLY

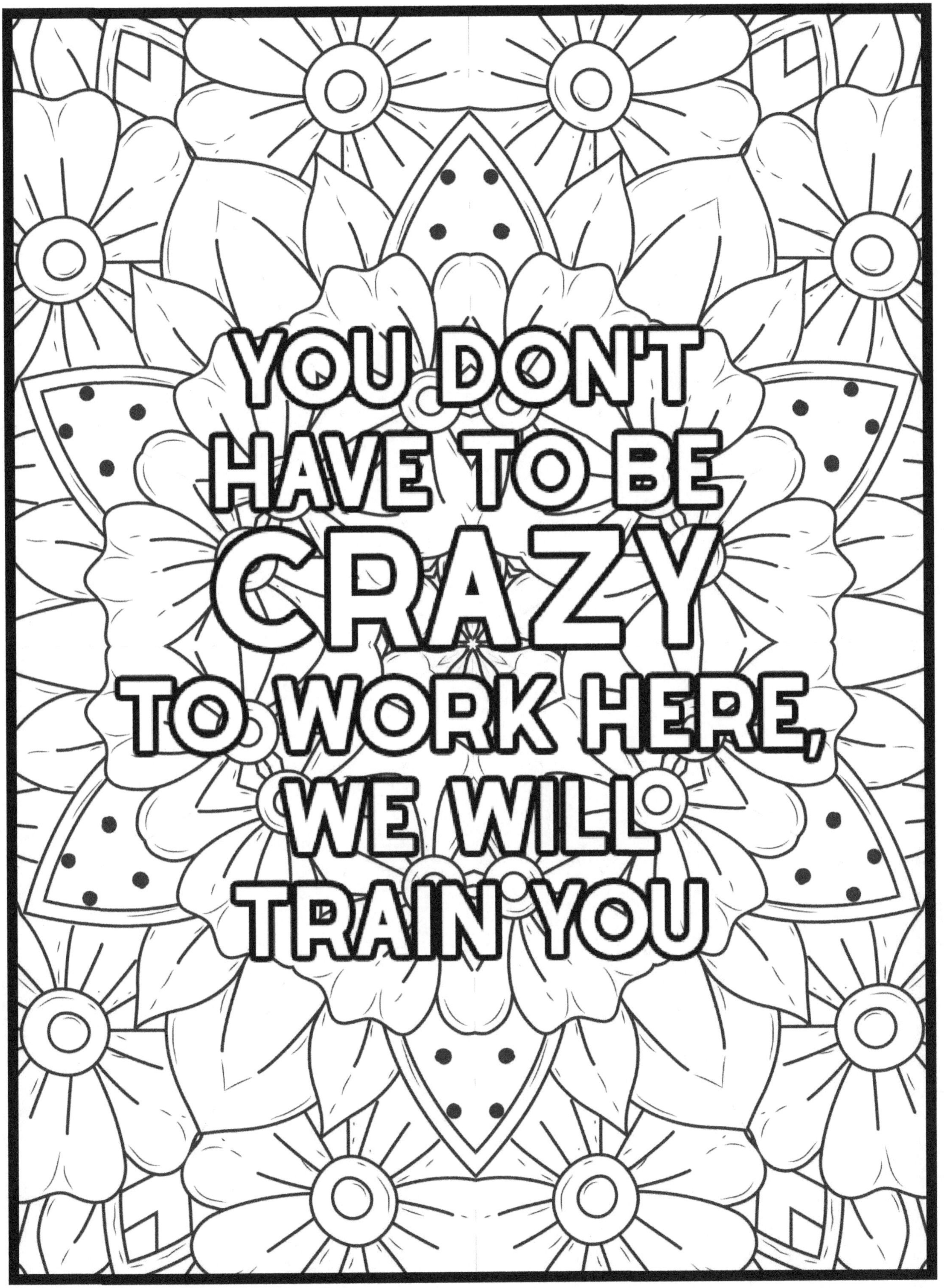
YOU DON'T
HAVE TO BE
CRAZY
TO WORK HERE,
WE WILL
TRAIN YOU

Nothing
surprises me
I work in
HR

WHAT
HAPPENS
IN HR
STAYS
IN HR

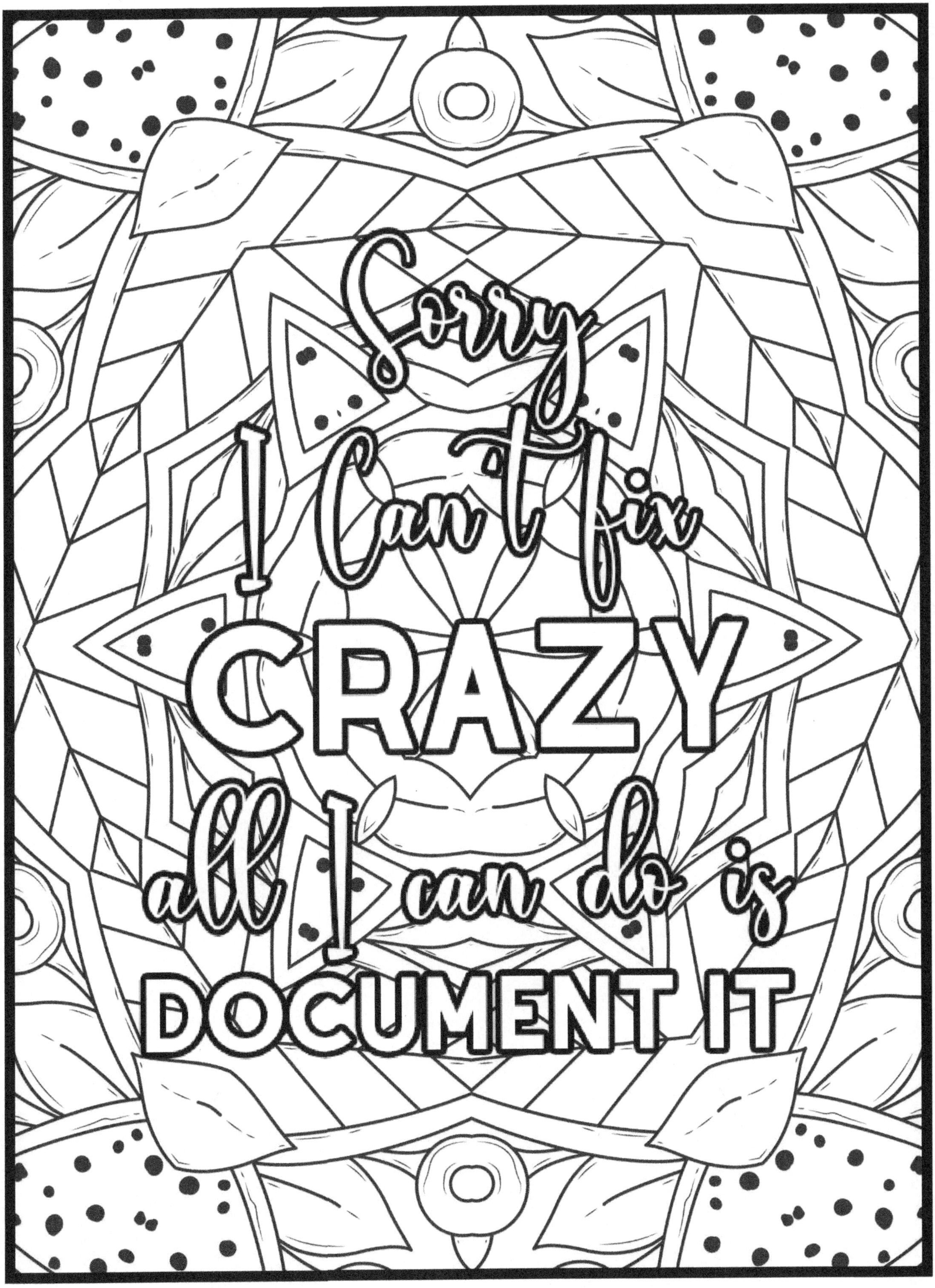
Sorry
I Can't fix
CRAZY
all I can do is
DOCUMENT IT

I'm an
HR
PROFESSIONAL.
what's your
SUPERPOWER?

I LOVE ASKING
EMPLOYEES
IF THEY HAVE
A MINUTE...
SCARES THEM
EVERY TIME

DON'T
MAKE ME
USE MY
HR
VOICE

I'M FINE
IT'S FINE
EVERYTHING
IS FINE

I NOTICE
EVERYTHING
I JUST
PRETEND
NOT TO

Made in the USA
Las Vegas, NV
12 December 2024

13950699R00031